Copyright Notice

@cardmakingcollective.com 2023

All Rights Reserved

No part of this website or any of its contents may be reproduced, copied, modified or adapted, without the prior written consent of the author, unless otherwise indicated for stand-alone materials.

Legal Notice

The author retains the right to change this guide at any time. This guide is for information purposes only and the author doesn't accept any responsibilities for any liabilities resulting from the use of this information. The reader assumes all responsibility for the use of the information herein.

Table of Contents

1. NEW BABY 4
2. GIRL BIRTHDAY 8
3. BOY BIRTHDAY 12
4. 16TH BIRTHDAY 16
5. 18TH BIRTHDAY 18
6. 21ST BIRTHDAY 20
7. 30TH BIRTHDAY 22
8. 40TH BIRTHDAY 24
9. 50TH BIRTHDAY 26
10. 60TH BIRTHDAY 28
11. 65TH BIRTHDAY 30
12. 70TH BIRTHDAY 32
13. 80TH BIRTHDAY 34
14. CHRISTMAS 36
15. EASTER 53
16. FATHER'S DAY 57
17. GENERIC CELEBRATIONS 61
18. GET WELL SOON 74
19. GRADUATION 78
20. MOTHER'S DAY 82
21. NEW HOUSE 87
22. RETIREMENT 91
23. SYMPATHY 95
24. THANK YOU 99
25. VALENTINES 103
26. WEDDING 107
27. SLIMLINE 111

Hi and welcome to *599 New & Inspiring Card Making Sketches!*

I'm Anna Lyons, founder of CardMakingCollective.com

If you've ever struggled with coming up with ideas for your cards, then this book will help!

Using sketches makes card making easy and fun, and they can save you time and give you lots of quick inspiration.

And sketches also leave lots of room for your own creativity too...

You see, a sketch simply tells you what goes where. And anyone who's spent hours trying to think of ideas knows how important that is.

But outside of the sketch, what color of card stock and embellishments you use is entirely up to you!

In fact, you could use the same sketch to create two totally different cards (just by choosing different colored and textured paper / embellishments).

I really hope you enjoy the inspiration and ideas within, and I wish you nothing but fun and excitement with your card making

Also – if you have any feedback or perhaps a testimonial about how *599 New And Inspiring Card Making Sketches* has helped you, I would love to hear from you.

Please email me using the contact us form on cardmakingcollective.com

Happy creating!

Anna Lyons

Anna Lyons
CardMakingCollective.com

P.S. Did you know we've got a book packed full of scrapbooking sketches too? For more information, go to our sister site, scrapbookingcoach.com

Chapter 1 - New Baby

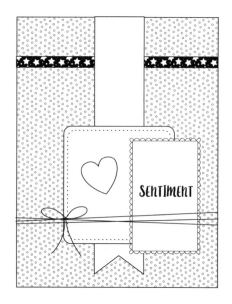
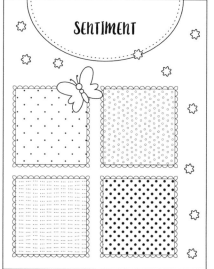

New Baby

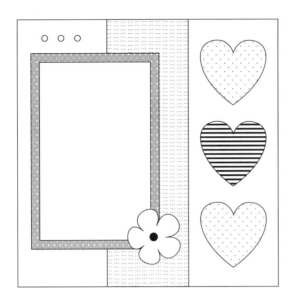

New Baby

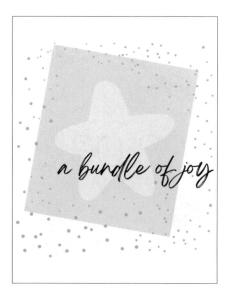
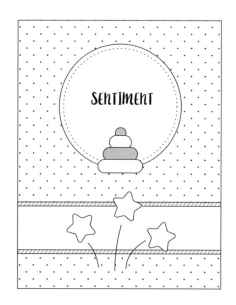

New Baby

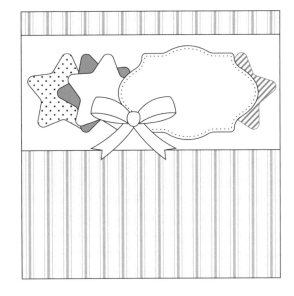

Chapter 2 - Girl Birthday

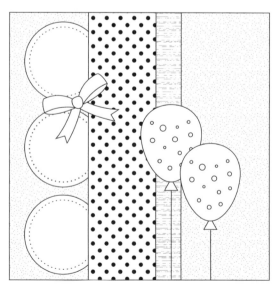

Girl Birthday

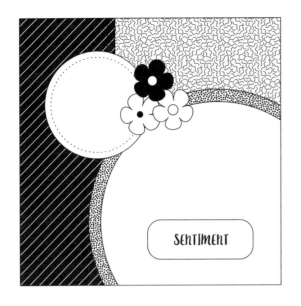
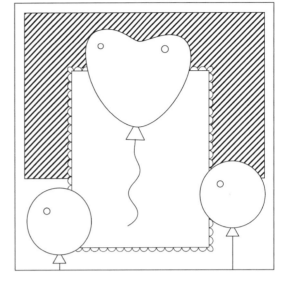

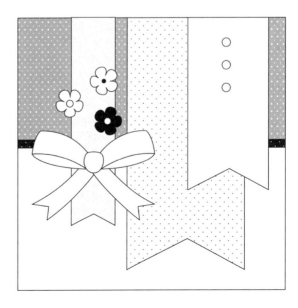

Girl Birthday

Girl Birthday

Chapter 3 – Boy Birthday

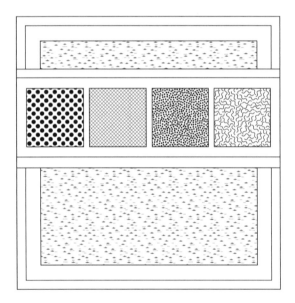

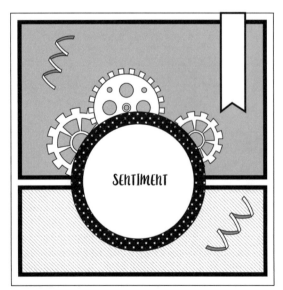
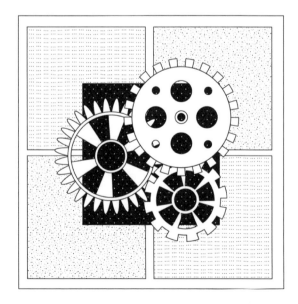

Boy Birthday

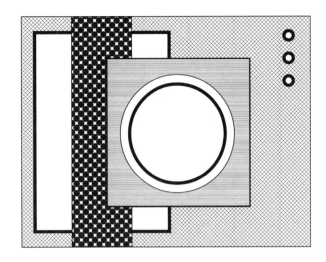

Boy Birthday

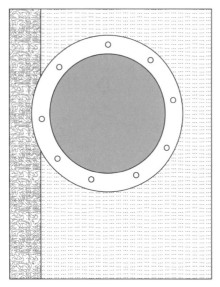
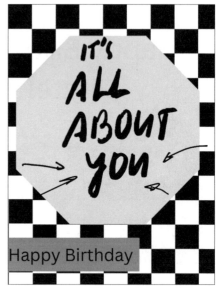
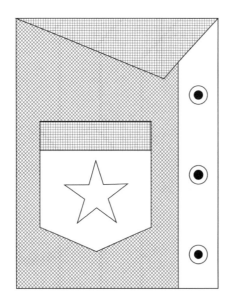
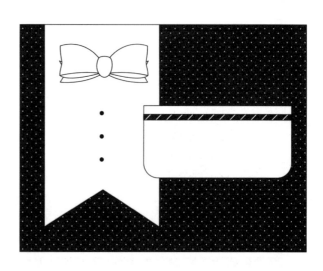

Boy Birthday

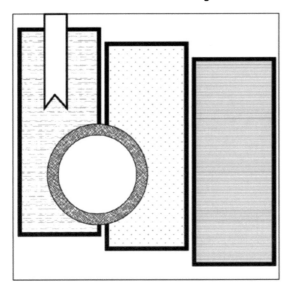
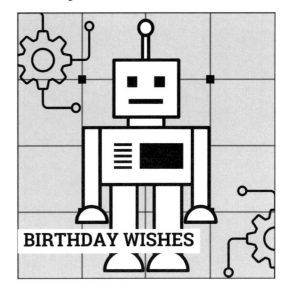

Chapter 4 - 16th Birthday

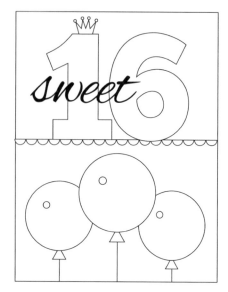

16th Birthday

Chapter 5 - 18th Birthday

18th Birthday

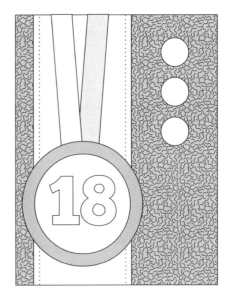

Chapter 6 - 21st Birthday

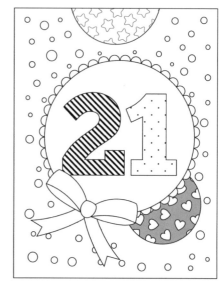

21st Birthday

Chapter 7 – 30th Birthday

30th Birthday

Chapter 8 - 40th Birthday

40th Birthday

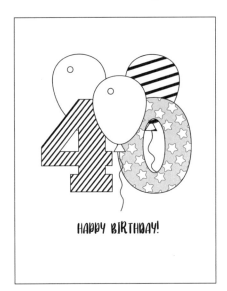

Chapter 9 – 50th Birthday

50th Birthday

Chapter 10 - 60th Birthday

60ᵗʰ Birthday

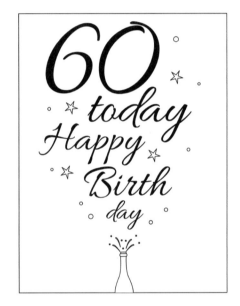

Chapter 11 - 65th Birthday

65th Birthday

Chapter 12 - 70th Birthday

70th Birthday

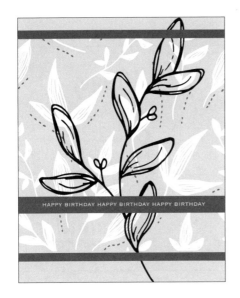

Chapter 13 – 80th Birthday

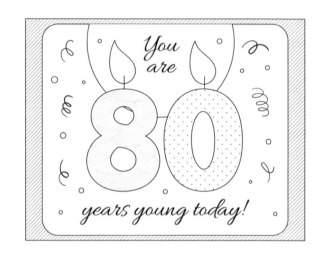

80th Birthday

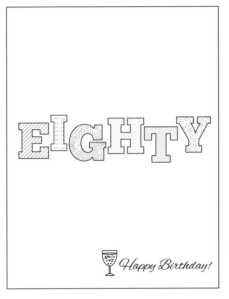

Chapter 14 - Christmas

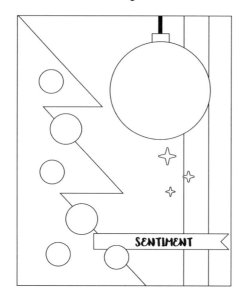
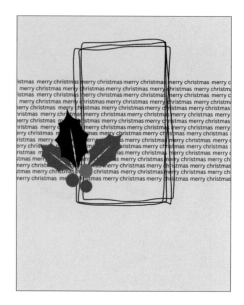

Christmas

Christmas

Christmas

Christmas

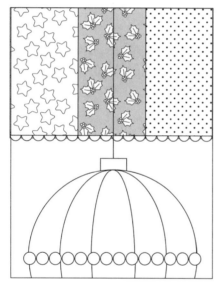
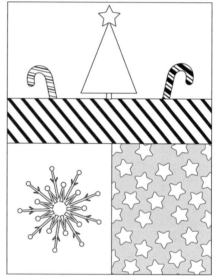

Christmas

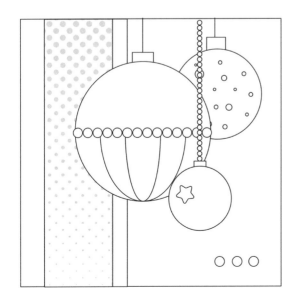

Christmas

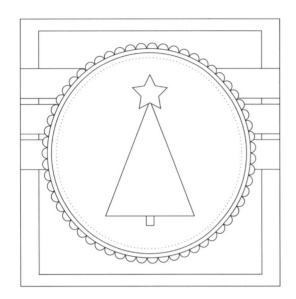

Christmas

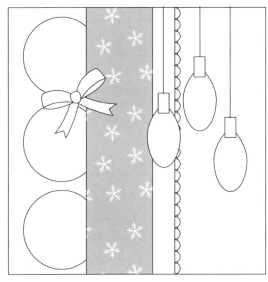

Christmas

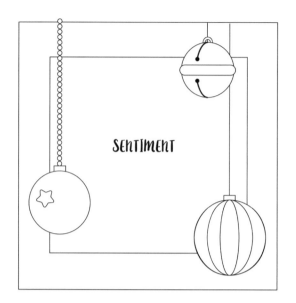

Christmas

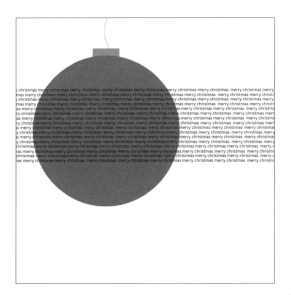

Christmas

Christmas

Christmas

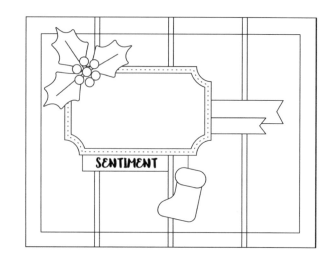
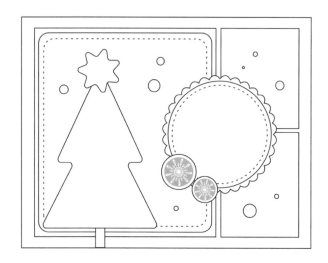

Christmas

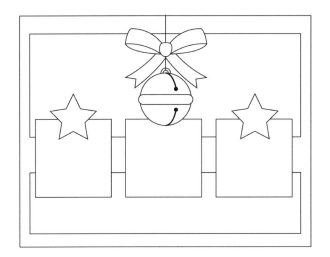

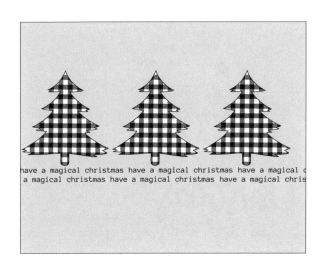
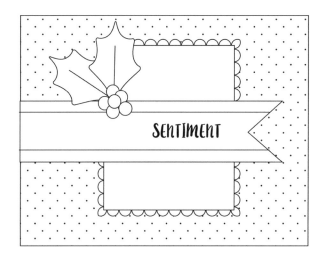

Christmas

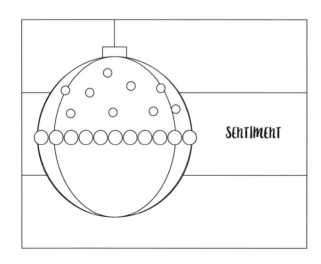

Christmas

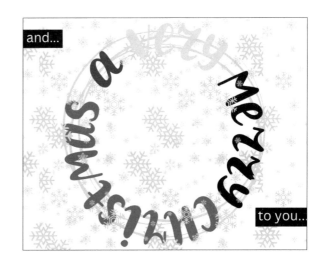

Christmas

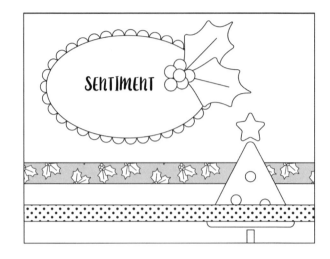
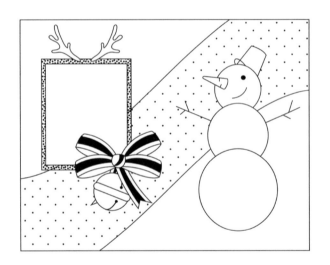
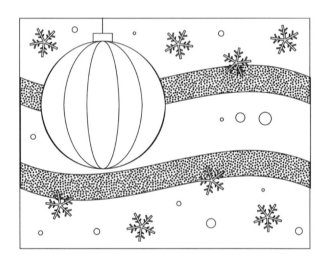

Chapter 15 - Easter

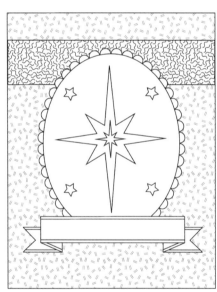

Easter

Easter

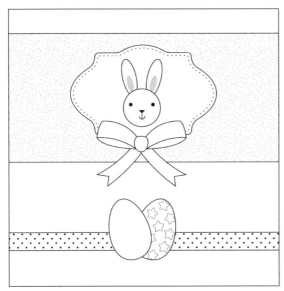

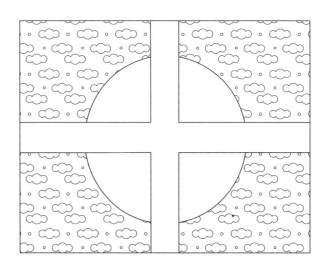

Easter

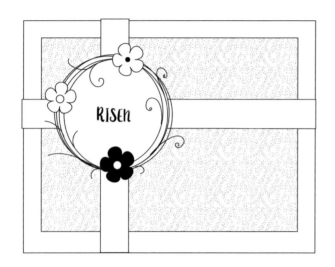

Chapter 16 - Father's Day

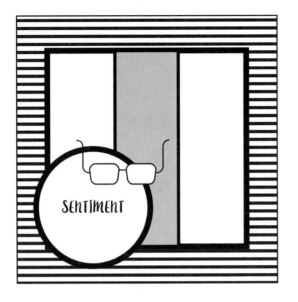

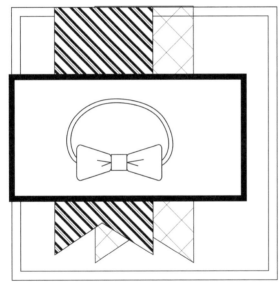
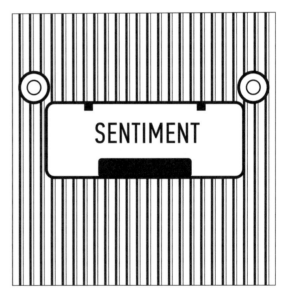

Father's Day

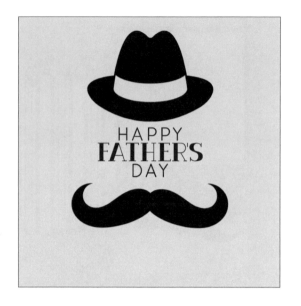

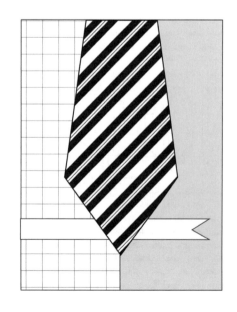

Father's Day

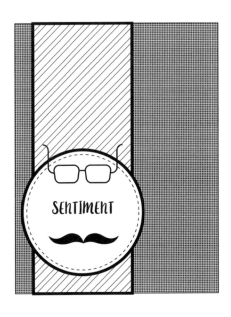

Father's Day

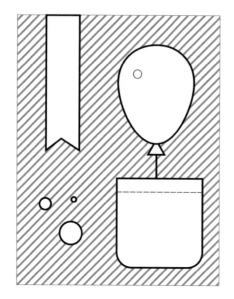 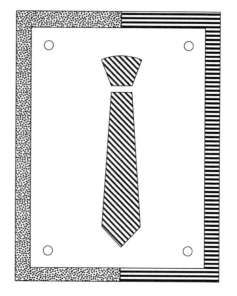

Chapter 17 - Generic Celebrations

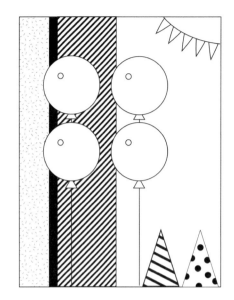

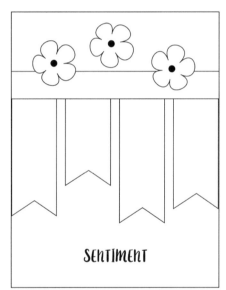

Generic Celebrations

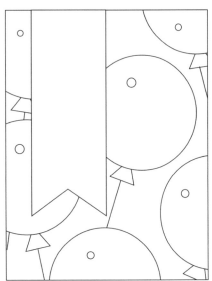

Generic Celebrations

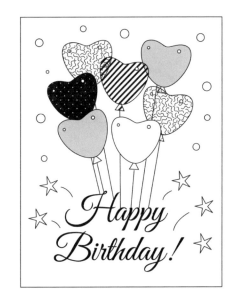

Generic Celebrations

Generic Celebrations

Generic Celebrations

Generic Celebrations

Generic Celebrations

Generic Celebrations

Generic Celebrations

Generic Celebrations

Generic Celebrations

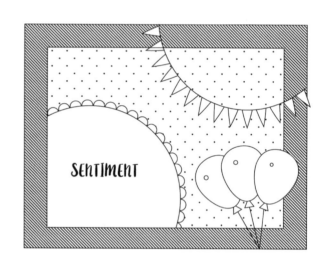
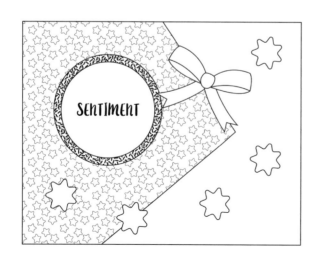

Generic Celebrations

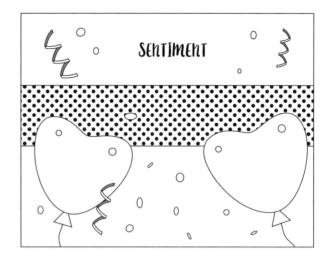

Chapter 18 - Get Well Soon

Get Well Soon

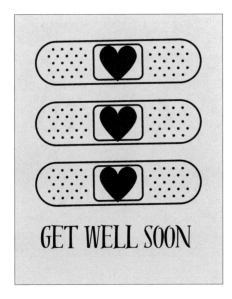

Get Well Soon

Get Well Soon

Chapter 19 - Graduation

1. go to uni ✓
2. pass exams ✓
3. graduate ✓

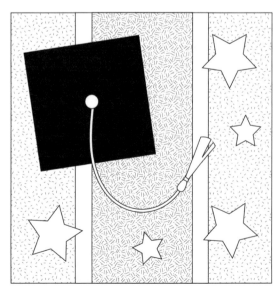

You did it!

Graduation

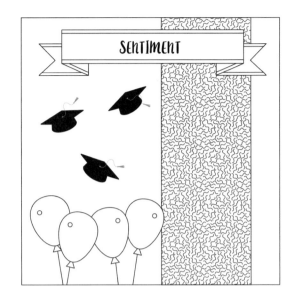

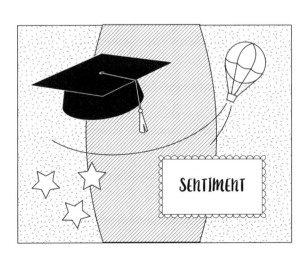

Graduation

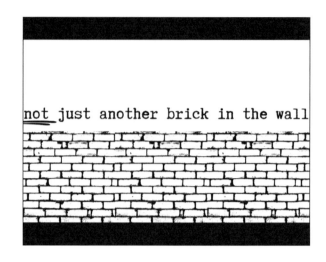

Graduation

Chapter 20 - Mother's Day

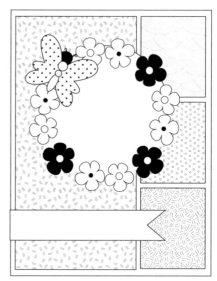

Mother's Day

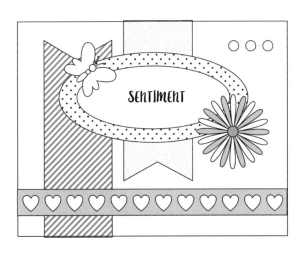

Mother's Day

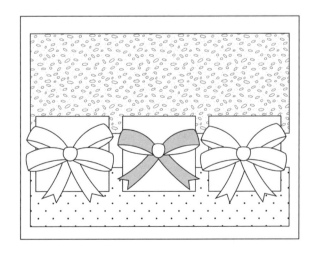

Mother's Day

Mother's Day

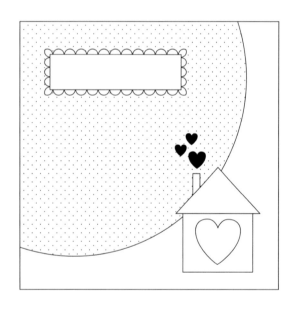

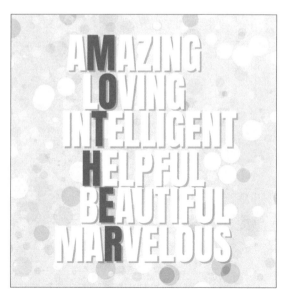

Chapter 21 - New House

New House

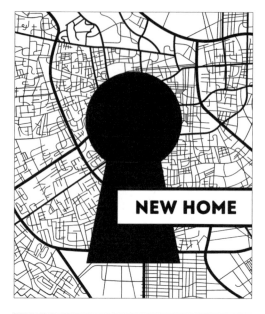

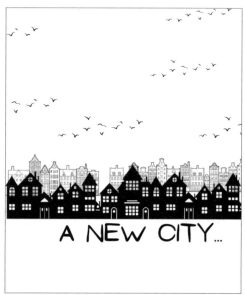

New House

New House

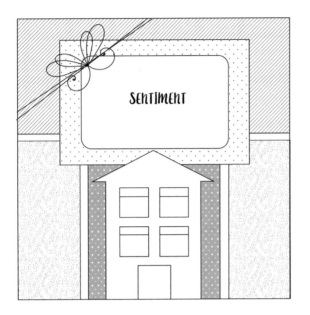

Chapter 22 - Retirement

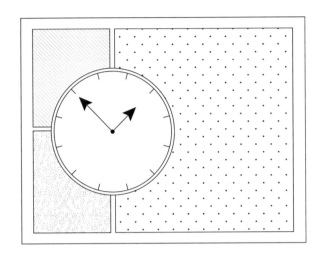

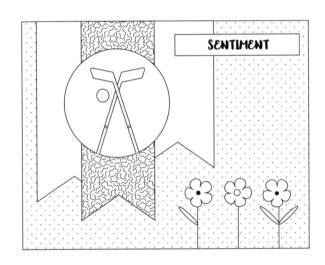
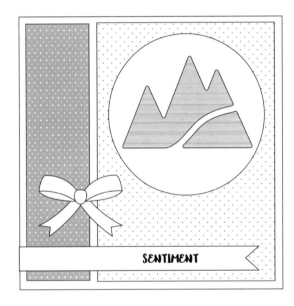
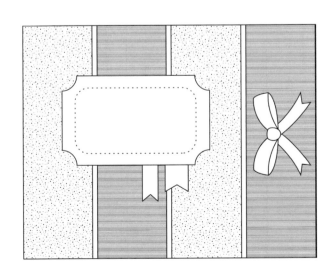

Retirement

Retirement

Retirement

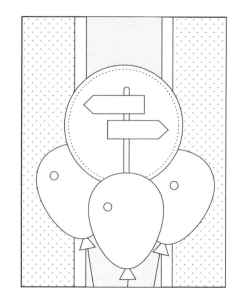

Chapter 23 - Sympathy

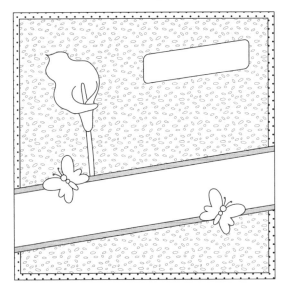

Sympathy

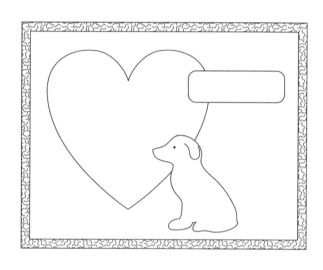

Sympathy

Sympathy

Chapter 24 - Thank You

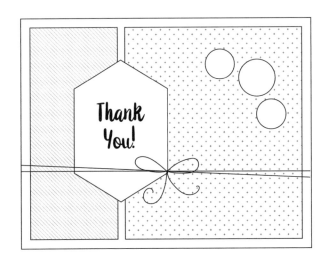

Thank You

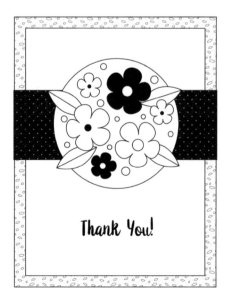

Thank You

Thank You

Chapter 25 - Valentines

Valentines

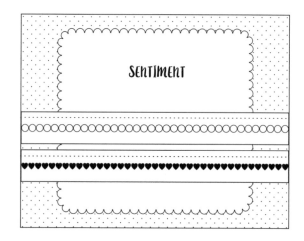

Valentines

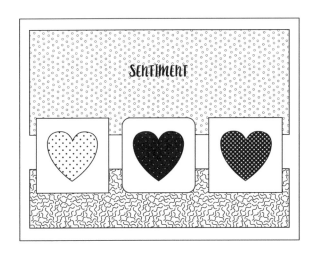

Valentines

Chapter 26 - Wedding Day

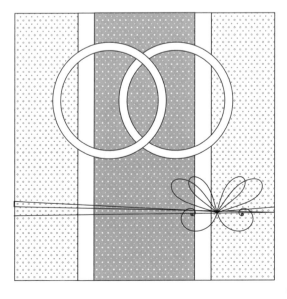

Wedding Day

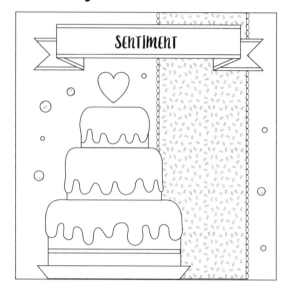

Wedding Day

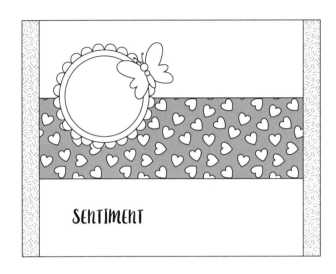

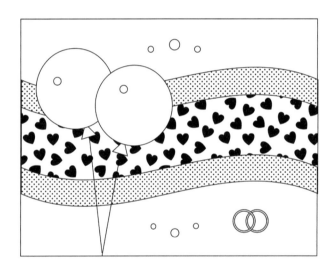

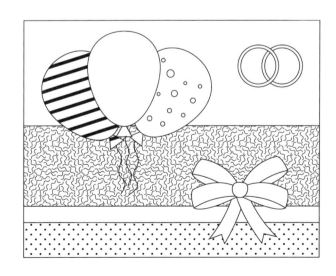

Wedding Day

Chapter 27 - Slimline

Slimline

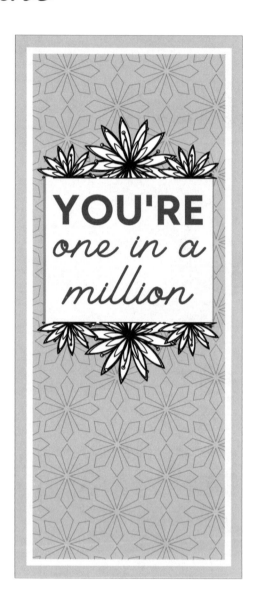

Slimline

Slimline

Slimline

Slimline

Slimline

Slimline

Slimline

Made in the USA
Columbia, SC
09 November 2023